CLASSICAL MUSIC FOR BANJO MADE EASY

Ondřej Šárek

The Vega Senator 5-string banjo image on the cover is courtesy of Deering Banjo Company.

© 2021 by Mel Bay Publications, Inc. All Rights Reserved.
WWW.MELBAY.COM

Preface

This book contains twenty well-known classical melodies arranged for 5-string banjo in G tuning. The selections span from the Baroque era to the beginning of the 20th century. All are set in standard notation and tablature in very easy melody/chord arrangements that rarely use the 5th string.

Some themes have been given a melodic treatment and can be played with the fingers in "classical banjo" style, or with picks in the 3-finger bluegrass style. Chord symbols are included so that the melodies may be accompanied by a guitarist, another banjo player or any other chord-capable instrument.

I hope this collection will provide some beautiful additions to your repertoire and improve your note-reading ability.

Ondřej Šárek

To my wonderful wife Jana, without whose family background
this book would not have been completed.

Contents

Title	Composer	Page
Preface		2
How to Read Tablature		5
An der schönen blauen Donau	Johann Strauss II (1825-1899)	6
Andělské přátelství	Adam Václav Michna z Otradovic (1600-1676)	8
Bridal Chorus	Richard Wagner (1813-1883)	9
Can-Can	Jacques Offenbach (1819-1880)	10
Caprice no. 24	Niccolò Paganini (1782-1840)	11
Das Wandern	Franz Schubert (1797-1828)	12
Ej, mamko, mamko	Leoš Janáček (1854-1928)	13
Gran Vals	Francisco Tárrega (1852-1909)	14
Humoresque	Antonín Dvořák (1841-1904)	16
Ja, das alles auf Ehr'	Johann Strauss II (1825-1899)	18
Kaiser-Walzer	Johann Strauss II (1825-1899)	19
La Donna è Mobile	Giuseppe Verdi (1813-1901)	20
Largo	Antonín Dvořák (1841-1904)	21
Lullaby	Johannes Brahms (1833-1897)	22
Melody	Anton Rubinstein (1829-1894)	23
Morning Mood	Edvard H. Grieg (1843-1907)	24
Sarabande	G. F. Händel (1685-1759)	25
Symphony No. 94 "Surprise"	Joseph Haydn (1732-1809)	26
Te Deum	Marc-Antoine Charpentier (1643-1704)	27
William Tell Overture	Gioacchino Rossini (1792-1868)	28

About the Author

Born in 1979, Ondřej Šárek earned a master's degree in Composition at The Janacek Academy of Music and Performing Arts while simultaneously studying Musicology at The Faculty of Arts at Masaryk University in Brno in the Czech Republic. An award-winning participant in several composition competitions, his chamber orchestra, symphonic and choral works are performed internationally. He has also written three mini-operas plus music for film, television, and theater productions.

As a skillful multi-instrumentalist, he devotes his time to playing and composing for piano, guitar, banjo, ukulele, Irish bouzouki, concertina, diatonic accordion, and mandola. He has arranged solo collections for various instruments, many of which have been released by Mel Bay Publications. Ondřej is also one of the leading arrangers of music for the ukulele, an instrument he hopes will regain its former prominence.

How to Read Tablature

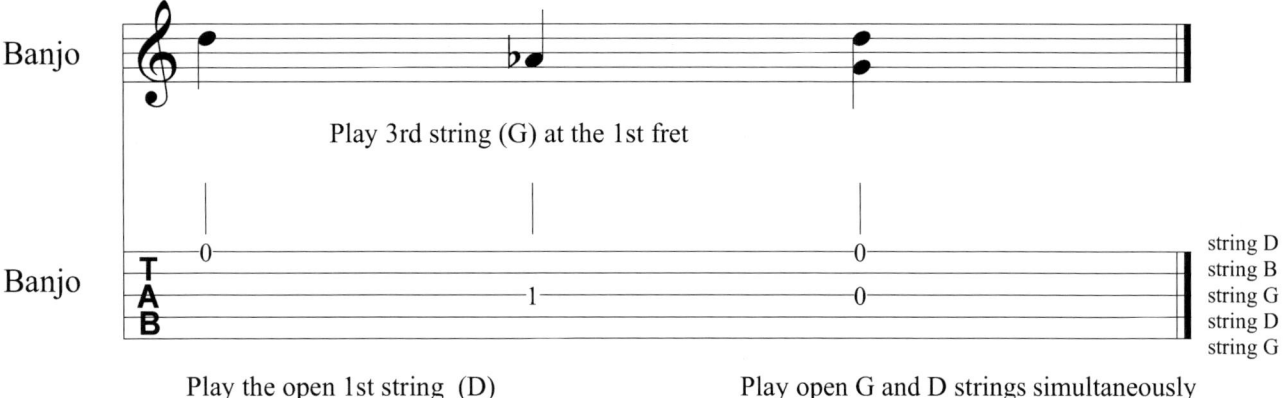

An der schönen blauen Donau

The Blue Danube Waltz

Johann Strauss II (1825-1899)

arr. Ondřej Šárek

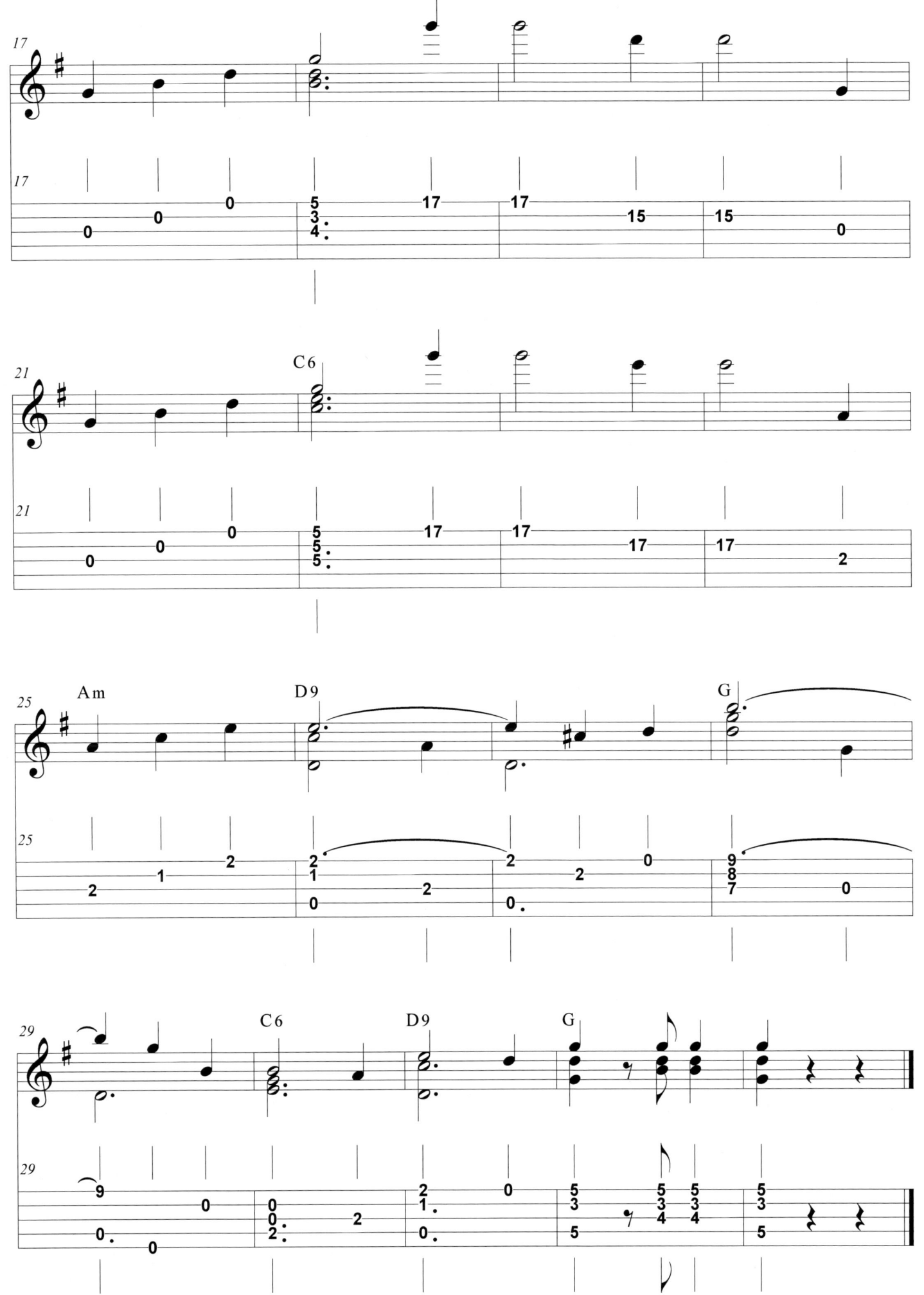

Andělské přátelství

Czech Baroque Hymn — Angelic Friendship — A.V. Michna (1600-1676), arr. Ondřej Šárek

Bridal Chorus

From the opera, *Lohengrin*

Richard Wagner (1813-1883)
arr. Ondřej Šárek

Can-Can

Orphée aux Enfers

Jacques Offenbach (1819-1880)

arr. Ondřej Šárek

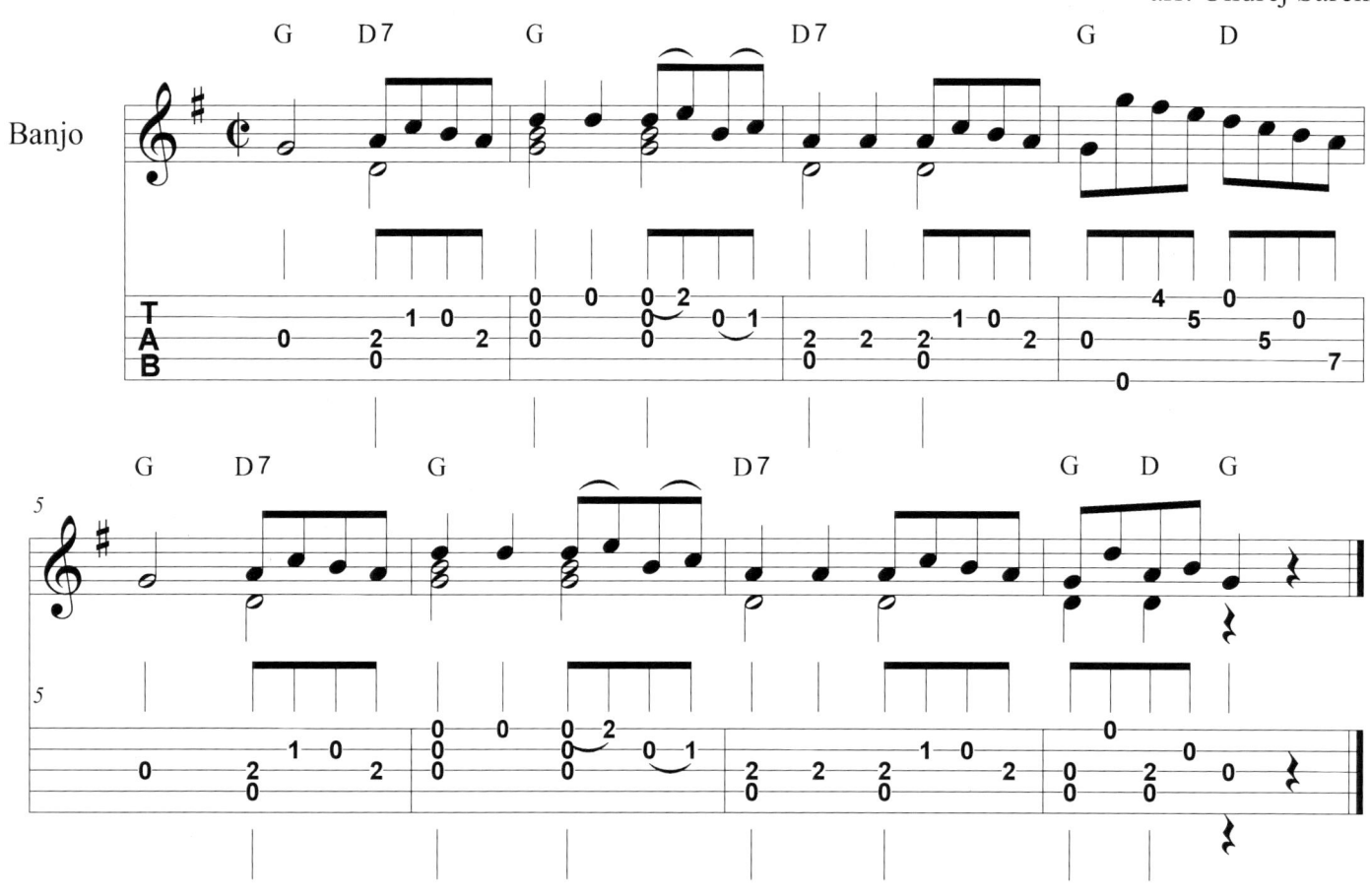

Caprice no. 24

Niccolò Paganini (1782-1840)
arr. Ondřej Šárek

Das Wandern

From the song cycle, *Die schöne Müllerin*

Franz Schubert (1797-1828)

arr. Ondřej Šárek

Ej, mamko, mamko

From the opera, *Její pastorkyňa*

Leoš Janáček (1854-1928)
arr. Ondřej Šárek

Gran Vals
Principal Theme

Francisco Tárrega (1852-1909)
arr. Ondřej Šárek

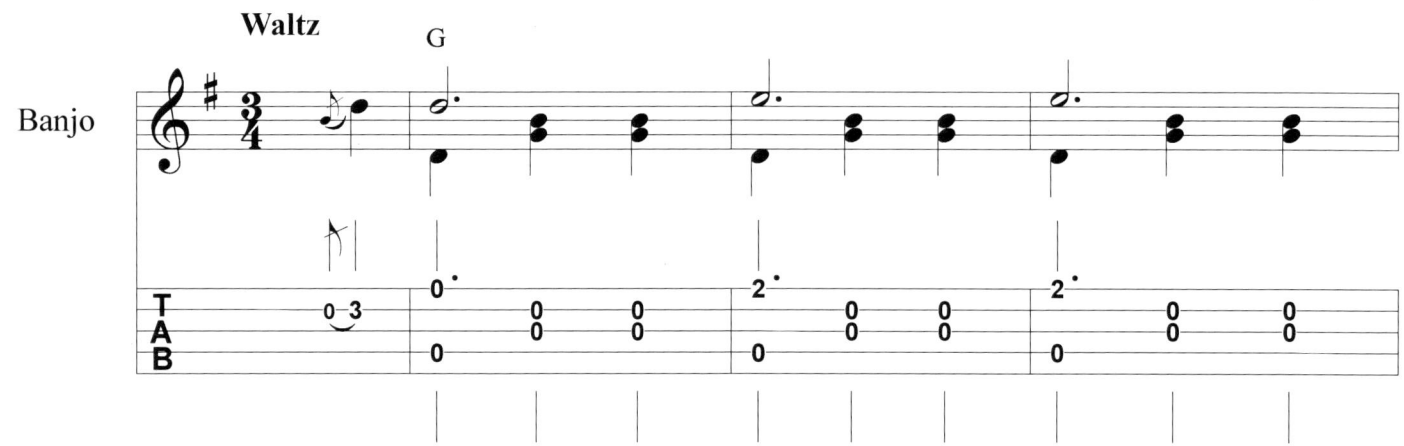
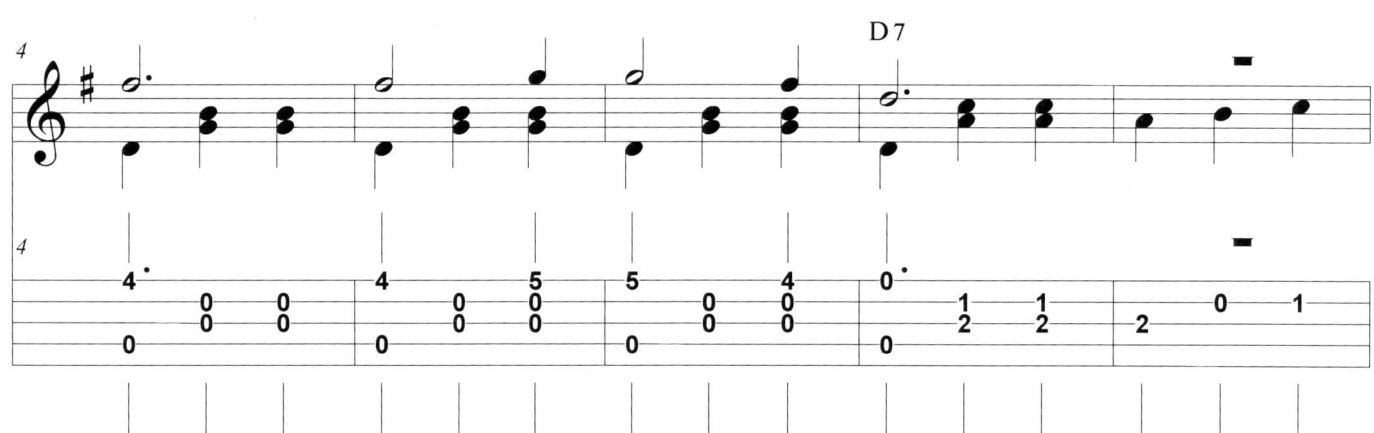
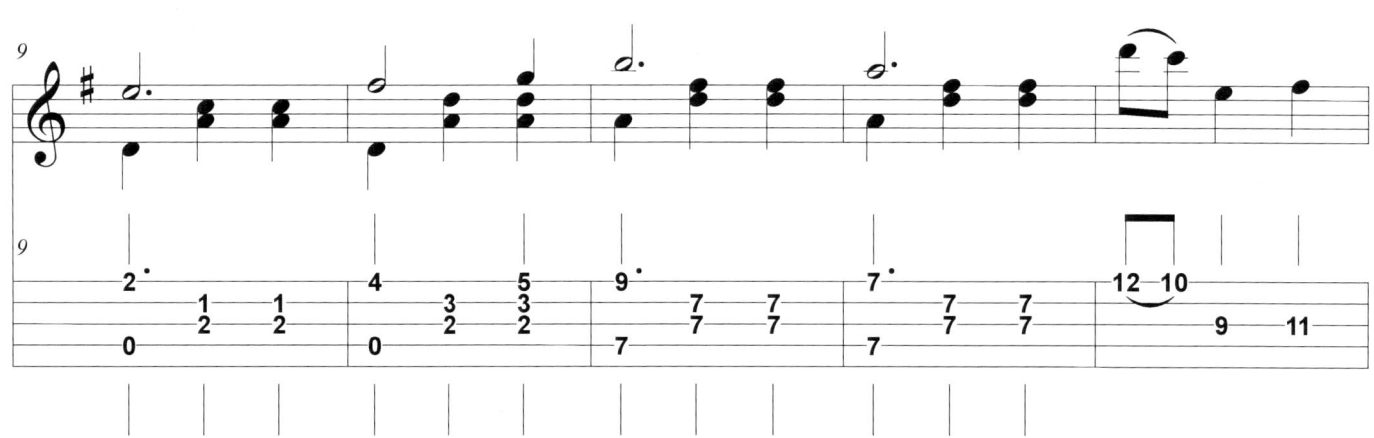

Humoresque
Principal Theme

Antonín Dvořák (1841-1904)
arr. Ondřej Šárek

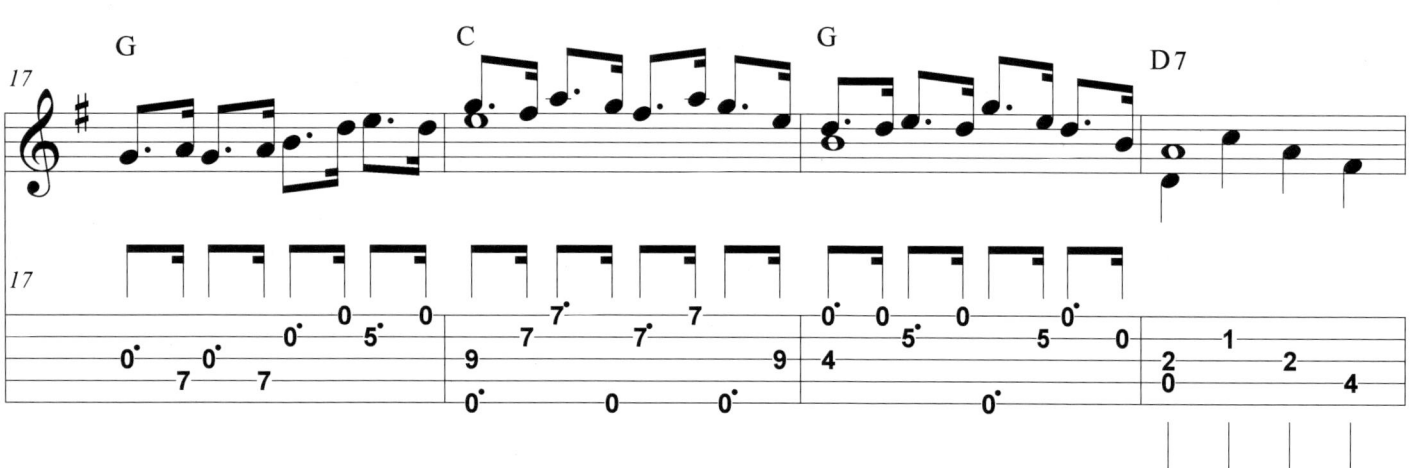
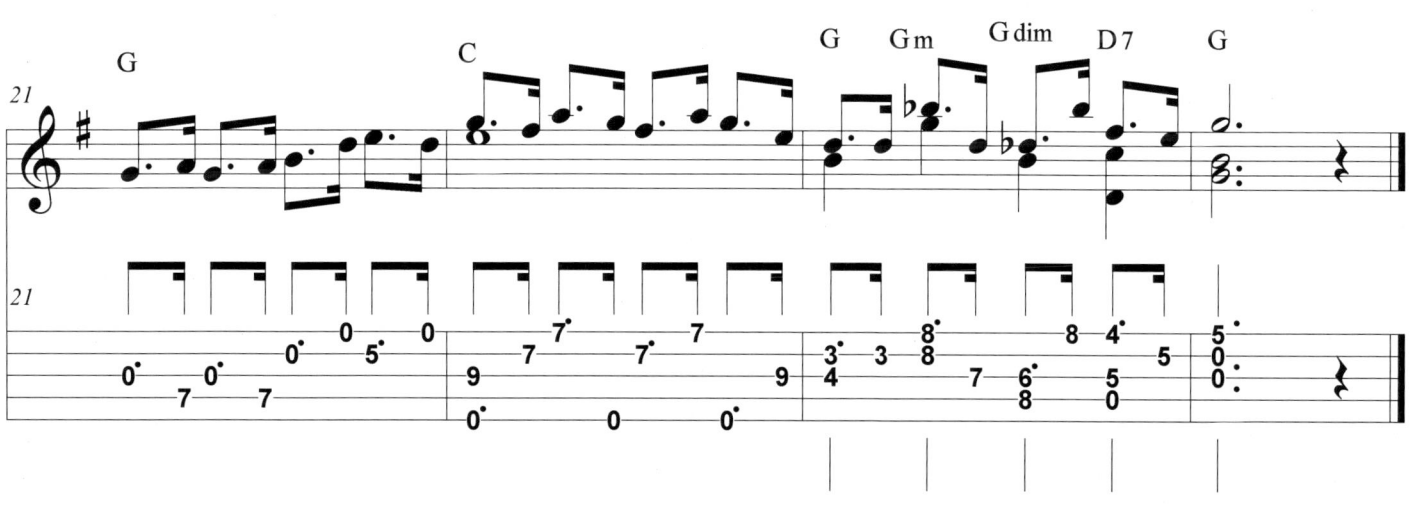

Ja, das alles auf Ehr'

Yes, on my honor

Johann Strauss II (1825-1899)
arr. Ondřej Šárek

Kaiser-Walzer

Johann Strauss II (1825-1899)
arr. Ondřej Šárek

La Donna è Mobile

From the opera, *Rigoletto*

Giuseppe Verdi (1813-1901)
arr. Ondřej Šárek

Largo

Theme from *Symphony No. 9*

Antonín Dvořák (1841-1904)
arr. Ondřej Šárek

Lullaby

Johannes Brahms (1833-1897)

arr. Ondřej Šárek

Melodie

Op. 3, No. 1

Anton Rubinstein (1829-1894)

arr. Ondřej Šárek

Morning Mood

From *Peer Gynt Suite*

Edvard H. Grieg (1843-1907)

arr. Ondřej Šárek

Symphony No. 94 "Surprise"

Theme, Second Movement

Joseph Haydn (1732-1809)
arr. Ondřej Šárek

Te Deum

Marc-Antoine Charpentier (1643-1704)

arr. Ondřej Šárek

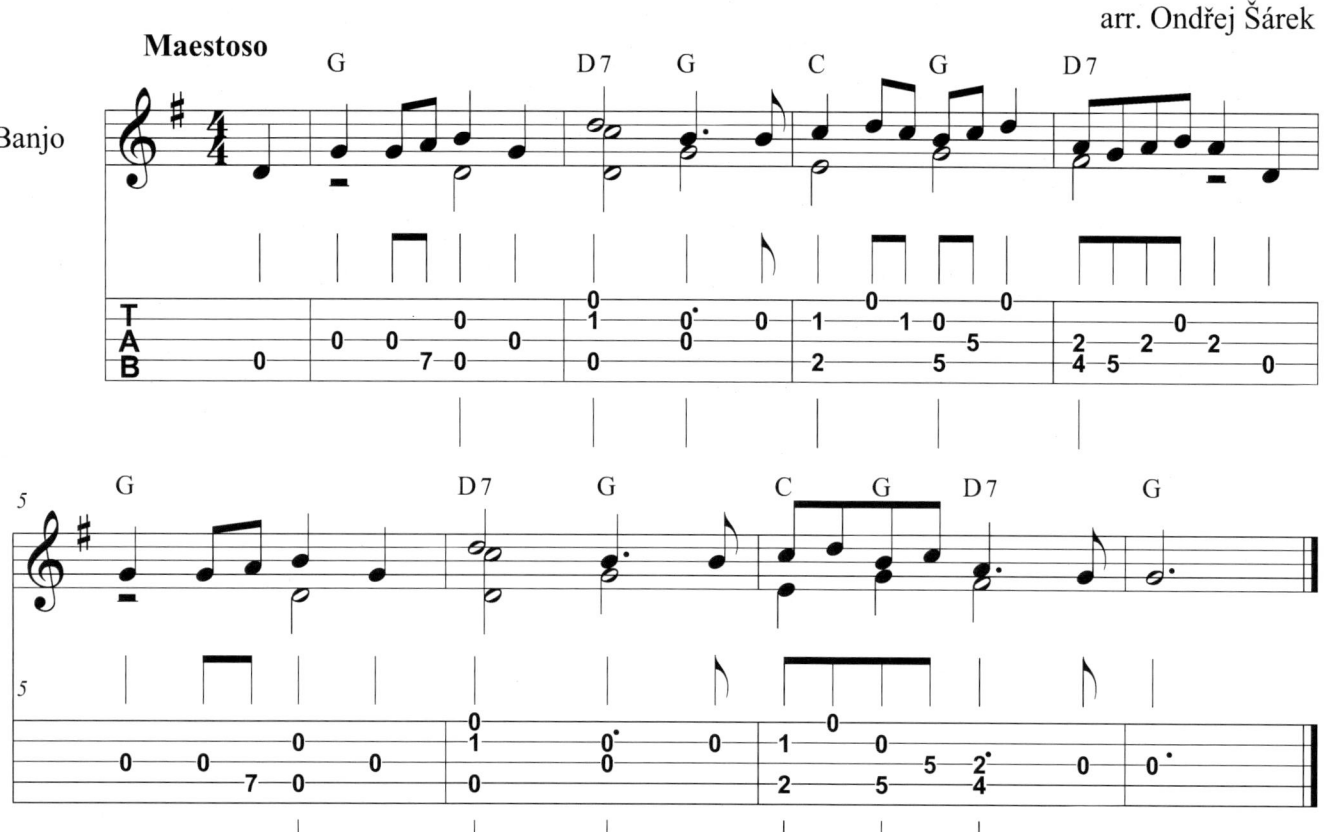

William Tell Overture

Principal Theme

Gioacchino Rossini (1792-1868)
arr. Ondřej Šárek